Attract Sell Keep: The Workbook

Exercises to Help You Learn

The Art of Marketing Your Services

By

Henry A. Feldman, Jr.

Copyright 2012

First Published by Create Space 01/06/2012.

ISBN-13: 978-1468154986
ISBN-10: 1468154982

Printed in the United States of America

Attract Sell Keep: The Workbook

Exercises to Help You Learn The Art of Marketing Your Services

"Skill to do comes of doing…"
Ralph Waldo Emerson, writer and poet

The following exercises reinforce the concepts and tools of ASK. They are organized to match the flow of the book so you can refer back to the chapters as you work.

Don't attempt to try and push through these exercises at one sitting or even over a weekend. You will have better results if you address two or three each week, doing a little work every day.

The first goal is to make marketing and selling a disciplined part of your daily routine. The second objective is to make these activities pleasureful.

Whether you use a spiral notebook, your laptop, or a smart phone to record your ideas and responses, date each page. Revisit what you wrote over time. You will be amazed at how valuable the content will be.

Before you begin, create an area just for ideas. I assure you, if you work these exercises faithfully, many ideas will come to you. Some you will want to act on; others you will discard. Either way, you want to collect them all.

Now take your time, sit back, and prepare your answers thoughtfully. Reading the book alone without doing the exercises won't cut the mustard.

Attract Sell Keep: The Workbook

ASK: A Roadmap to Attract, Sell, Keep

Section 1: Attract

Attracting new business requires service professionals to actively offer services that stir potential buyers' interest to contact them. It is then up to the professional to close the sale, provide the promised services, solve a problem, or satisfy a need. Professionals must provide services in such a way that they build their reputations as competent, trustworthy, and likable providers. To attract prospects requires ongoing market research, planning, experimentation, and creativity.

EXERCISES for Attracting New Business

1. Describe the type of service business you would like to build over the next five years by answering these questions:

    a. What services would you **prefer** to offer?

    _____

    _____

    _____

    _____

    _____

    _____

    b. What kind of customers/patients/clients would you **prefer** to serve?

    _____

    _____

    _____

    _____

    _____

    _____

    _____

c. Where would you **prefer** to be located?

_____

_____

_____

_____

_____

_____

_____

d. How many hours per week are you **prepared** to work?

_____

_____

_____

_____

_____

_____

_____

e. What are your **personal** priorities?

_____

_____

_____

_____

_____

_____

_____

f. What makes you think these decisions will continue to **delight** you?

_____

_____

_____

_____

_____

_____

_____

g. How much **money** would you like to be making in five years?

_____

_____

_____

_____

_____

_____

_____

2. **Describe the characteristics of your target market, the people you
    would primarily like to serve.** Make your list as specific as possible.
    Some examples: age range, gender, location, ethnicity, language, level
    of education, type of organization, or level of wealth.

_____

_____

_____

_____

_____

_____

3. **What problems does your target market have that you can solve?**
Finding an unmet need or a problem not solved for prospects at a price they are willing and able to pay is a great way to accelerate the growth of your business. Ask clients and prospects what their problems are. As they talk take notes in your notebook and then come up with the services they are seeking.

_____

_____

_____

_____

_____

_____

_____

4. **Describe the buying habits of your target market. If you don't know, go ask them.** Talk to others who provide similar services to the people you want to serve. Search the Internet to identify research that has been done regarding the ways your market segment buys both services and products.

_____

_____

_____

_____

_____

_____

_____

_____

_____

5. **Describe your service offerings.** Detail the specific services you provide. Include what you will and will not do. Select the services that address the unique requirements of your chosen market.

_____

_____

_____

_____

_____

_____

_____

_____

_____

_____

6. **What financial, experiential, and/or personal hurdles must you surmount before you can effectively launch your marketing program?** List these challenges. These hurdles may be acquiring a bank or Small Business Administration loan or getting more experience from your current employer; acquiring another educational degree or professional license; saving enough money to buy equipment to open your office, or getting enthusiastic support from your spouse and family.

7. **Identify specific tasks you can do now to start the process of addressing these hurdles.** Prepare a task list, the more specific the better. This list will put details to your responses to Question 6. Some examples: Matriculate at the local college to get a Certified Financial Planning™ certificate; set aside ten percent of your monthly salary to make a meaningful down payment on equipment; arrange a meeting with complementary professionals such as potential business partners, customers, or referral sources, to explore possible relationships, or hire a business coach, psychologist, or computer expert for needed counsel.

8. **Get to know your local competitors.** Gather information on how they attract business, their services, and if possible, how they structure their fees. Collect their brochures. Visit their websites. Subscribe to their newsletters, blogs, or RSS feeds. Find ways to get to know your competitors personally. Take notes. From this gathered intelligence, start noting what you need to do to differentiate your business. Especially consider what you can do that a competitor can't.

_____

_____

_____

_____

_____

_____

_____

_____

9. **What services can you offer that differentiate you from your competitors?** Write down point by point the differences. Figure out how to express these differences positively, without referring to or disparaging the competition.

_____

_____

_____

_____

_____

_____

_____

_____

_____

_____

10. **How might you discover new services to offer your targeted market?** Join a national or local industry association. Peers from other communities are often happy to help. Review the journals, blogs, and emails written by others in your field, especially those published outside your local area.

_____

_____

_____

_____

_____

_____

_____

_____

11. **How do you set your prices?** Why did you choose this method?
    Is it based on your costs, what the competition is charging, or what you
    think your services are worth? Does your pricing reflect the quality or
    composition of the services or is it a guess-timate? Are you using your
    offering price to attract all customers (McDonald's), to attract a select
    few (Tiffany), to maximize your profits, or to stick to the middle-of-the-
    road so price is not the disqualifying point?

    _____

    _____

    _____

    _____

    _____

    _____

    _____

12. **Think about the fears, biases, and other psychological inhibitors
    that may be preventing you from actively promoting your
    services.** Make a list. Next to each write down what you can do to
    overcome it. Be honest, only you have to see what you write.

    _____

    _____

    _____

    _____

    _____

_____

_____

_____

_____

_____

_____

_____

_____

13. **Are there prohibitions in your industry or any legal restrictions regarding marketing your services?** If you don't know, do a little research. If there are restrictions, write them down. If your page is blank, you are free to fly. Most professionals discover that any restrictions are minimal and will not interfere with marketing efforts.

_____

_____

_____

_____

_____

_____

14. What constitutes an assertive right? List the assertive rights that feel "right" to you. Mark those that you practice regularly, those that you practice sometimes, and those you don't practice at all. Are you missing marketing and sales opportunities because you are aren't practicing all your assertive rights?

_____

_____

_____

_____

_____

_____

_____

_____

_____

_____

_____

_____

_____

_____

15. Develop a three sentence (or less) answer to the question: "What do you do for a living?" Prepare a short elevator speech that is interesting without bragging. Repeat it out loud until it is smooth and automatic. Example: "I help large companies materially reduce their annual telephone costs."

16. List your favorite customers and describe how you initially attracted each one. Next to each name record how they discovered you, for example a referral, a random inquiry, telephone inquiry, Internet, direct mail, etc. This is about them finding you; not about you finding them. Define a process to help you replicate those successes.

_____

_____

_____

_____

_____

_____

_____

_____

_____

_____

_____

_____

_____

_____

17. **List possible long-and short-term strategies to attract greater interest in your services.** Long-term strategies might be getting an advanced degree or special license; learning another language if you are in the travel business; moving to another, more vital city, or forming a marketing cooperative. Short-term strategies might be volunteering to support a local not-for-profit; taking a speed-reading course; meeting the various directors of a local foundation, or investing in a more stylish wardrobe.

_____

_____

_____

_____

_____

_____

_____

_____

_____

_____

_____

_____

_____

18. **How could you introduce your services for little or no cost?** For example, offer a free DVD that shows how you do your work or permit a potential reader to review the first two chapters of your book.

_____

_____

_____

_____

_____

19. **What can you do to convincingly demonstrate to your market that you are an expert in your field?** Add new licenses or certifications. Teach part time at a respected college or university. Build a relationship with key reporters in the local media so they know to contact you when they need help to write a story about your industry. Author articles or even write a book. You can become an adjunct professor at a local college or teach a continuing education course.

_____

_____

_____

_____

_____

20. **What would you do if you wanted to quickly promote a news item that reflected favorably on your business?** What would you do if you had won a prestigious award, were about to give a speech, had published an article about innovations in your field, or were announcing a unique service? List the tactics and/or tools you might use to get news out to your market in an inexpensive, timely, and professional way.

\
\
\
\
\
\
\

21. **If someone asked you to send them information about your business, how would you efficiently respond?** Write down the questions that you would ask to qualify this lead. What material would you send? In your notebook, develop a repeatable process that will allow you to send out marketing materials efficiently.

\
\
\
\
\

22. Where might you advertise so your targeted market can see your logo/brand on a regular basis? List the media opportunities in your area. Can you place an ad in the local newspaper, on a billboard, or sponsor a local sports team?

_____

_____

_____

_____

_____

_____

23. What can you say about your services that would be notable or add credibility to your business? For example, "*Doing Business in Glencoe since 1942,*" "*Specializing in Painting Victorian Homes,*" or "*Only Firm on the North Shore Offering Plumbing Services 24/7.*"

_____

_____

_____

_____

_____

_____

24. How might a public relations expert quickly introduce your business to your community? Find someone with experience in your field to propose a marketing strategy for you.

_____

_____

_____

_____

_____

_____

_____

25. Building your referral strategy.

a. List ways you can deepen the relationships you have with your family, friends, customers, and centers-of-influence. People who really like and respect you are the ones most likely to make referrals.

_____

_____

_____

_____

_____

_____

_____

b. List other businesses and professionals that could become productive referral sources. Include them in your lead generation strategy,

_____

_____

_____

_____

_____

_____

c. Refer back to your list of existing customers and how they came to your business. What percentage of your business is from referrals? Who were the most productive referrers?

_____

_____

_____

_____

_____

_____

_____

_____

d. The various tactics and tools needed to achieve your referral strategies.

_____

_____

_____

_____

_____

_____

_____

26. After reading Chapter 7, write a simple business plan describing briefly:

a. Your mission statement

_____

_____

_____

_____

_____

_____

_____

25

b. Long-term career goals

_____

_____

_____

_____

_____

_____

c. The main strategies chosen to acheive those future goals, and

_____

_____

_____

_____

_____

_____

_____

_____

d. The various tactics and tools needed to achieve those strategies.

_____

_____

_____

_____

_____

_____

27. **Make a punch-list of the specific tasks to complete before you launch your marketing program.** These may include: creating a website; preparing a trifold; identifying other professionals you might need to provide legal, accounting and other technical skills, and deciding on a target market to pursue. Set deadlines for each task and make sure you meet them.

_____

_____

_____

_____

_____

_____

Attract Sell Keep: The Workbook
ASK: A Roadmap to Attract, Sell, Keep

Section 2: Sell

Selling is a subset of marketing. In the ASK methodology, selling services begins the moment the initial contact between a seller and prospect occurs and ends when the prospect decides whether or not to hire someone. The ethical selling of services involves the seller identifying and then solving the buyers' problems or satisfying their needs. In return, the buyer pays a fair price for the value received. Ethical selling is not a battle between eager sellers trying to manipulate reluctant buyers into purchasing unwanted solutions or opportunistic buyers trying to solve their problems without paying for the value they receive.

EXERCISES for Creating Profitable Business Relationships

THE QUALIFICATION PROCESS

Qualifying prospects before you meet them saves you time by identifying the "best" prospects for your business.

1. **Taking into consideration the profile of your ideal client, list the questions you could ask that would:**

    a. Identify desirable prospects.

    _____

    _____

    _____

    _____

    _____

    _____

    b. Screen out undesirable prospects.

    _____

    _____

    _____

    _____

    _____

    _____

c. Establish shared expectations of your ability to solve the customer's problem.

_____

_____

_____

_____

_____

_____

_____

2. **Describe what you can do to redirect low probability or undesirable prospects elsewhere without harming your reputation.**

_____

_____

_____

_____

_____

_____

_____

3. List the names of five to ten professionals you have used in the past few years. After each name list:

a. How did you discover them?

_____

_____

_____

_____

_____

_____

_____

_____

_____

_____

_____

_____

_____

_____

b. How much time did you spend performing due diligence to determine if they were qualified to meet your needs?

_____

_____

_____

_____

_____

c. How happy are you with their services?

_____

_____

_____

_____

_____

d. What did you discover by doing this exercise?

_____

_____

_____

_____

_____

4. **What admirable attributes do you seek when you interview potential service providers?** How would you compare your sales approach to those you admire?

   _____

   _____

   _____

   _____

   _____

   _____

5. **What types of sales behaviors turn you off?** Be specific when you try to recollect your personal experiences.

   _____

   _____

   _____

   _____

   _____

   _____

   _____

6. **If you were to write a Code of Conduct for your business what ethical principles would you insist everyone follow?** Create one that would make you proud of what you are doing.

_____

_____

_____

_____

_____

_____

7. **List at least three reasons why it is in _your best interest_ to maintain high ethical standards when marketing and selling.**

_____

_____

_____

_____

_____

_____

8. **List three examples of unethical behavior or practices that you have observed in your industry.**

_____

_____

_____

_____

_____

_____

9. **How can you prevent these unethical practices from infecting your company?** How can you as an ethical seller demonstrate your trustworthiness? Some examples are: offering a money-back guarantee; providing full disclosure of potential risks, or not accepting business if you think it is in the prospect's best interest to go elsewhere.

_____

_____

_____

_____

_____

_____

THE SELLING PROCESS

When you clearly understand what it takes to go from initial call to signed agreement, you will be able to balance your resources and close more sales. The following exercises will help you map a sales process tailored to your business.

1. **How do you currently prepare for the first meeting with a prospect?** Write down the steps you typically take before you meet with a prospect. For example, do you look up information on the Internet to learn more about her business, ask the referrer for additional insights, or try another investigative approach?

_____

_____

_____

_____

_____

_____

_____

_____

_____

_____

_____

2. **What kind of a total impression do you want to make?** Ask a trusted friend for honest feedback. Does your appearance match the customer's expectations? Are you creating the impression that will cause a prospect to have confidence in your ability to help?

_____

_____

_____

_____

_____

_____

3. **What can you do to establish emotional rapport so your prospects relax and believe that you are competent, trustworthy, and likable?** Establishing rapport is an essential component of any successful first meeting and requires that sellers adjust their behavior and communications for each unique prospect. It is important to trust your instincts, listen carefully, respond honestly, and make an active effort to show you care about solving the prospect's problem.

_____

_____

_____

_____

_____

_____

_____

_____

_____

_____

4. **Looking back to previous customer opportunities, what five or so information gathering questions were most productive in identifying the problem or the need?** This is a good time to review the detailed notes you made during previous meetings with prospects. If you aren't in the habit of taking notes, build that into your sales process now.

_____

_____

_____

_____

_____

_____

_____

_____

_____

5. **Do the questions you ask get the prospects to openly discuss their problems?** Once you have established some rapport, ask the questions that will allow you to accurately define the prospect's need or problem. How might you improve your questioning technique?

_____

_____

_____

_____

_____

_____

6. **What other questions can you ask to persuade prospects to think deeper about why they came to see you?** What can you do when the prospect is hesitant about divulging information or remains non-responsive? Come up with a list of questions that may cause the prospect to think deeper about why they came to see you. How will you ask why he or she appears hesitant or evasive about answering your questions if that appears to be the case?

_____

_____

_____

_____

_____

_____

7. **Make a list of your significant accomplishments (brags) that would impress a prospect about your competence.** Practice the art of gently sprinkling your accomplishments into your conversation so they don't seem boastful. Hang your awards, citations, and degrees on your office walls. Include them on panel two of your trifold.

_____

_____

_____

_____

_____

_____

_____

_____

_____

_____

_____

_____

_____

8. **If a second meeting is required, prepare a follow-up letter that consists of:**

   a. Your appreciation for the prospect taking time to meet with you;

   b. A restatement of what you believe to be the the problem or need they are trying to address;

   c. What you are planning to accomplish at the next meeting;

   d. The time and date for the next meeting, and

   e. A reminder of the importance of having all decision makers present at the next meeting.

   Mail this letter as soon as possible after the meeting to avoid losing the goodwill you created at the first meeting. Draft a sample letter here.

   _____

   _____

   _____

   _____

   _____

   _____

   _____

   _____

   _____

9. **If the sale requires that you make a formal proposal, what are the essential elements of your proposal?** List them and explain why they are essential.

_____

_____

_____

_____

_____

_____

_____

_____

_____

_____

_____

_____

_____

_____

10. How would you prioritize your recommendations and why?

a. List your most profitable service.

_____

_____

_____

_____

_____

_____

b. List the services you provide that are most likely to be accepted.

_____

_____

_____

_____

_____

_____

_____

_____

_____

c. How do you prioritize your service recommendations to increase the probability of being hired?

_____

_____

_____

_____

_____

_____

_____

d. Why is it important to ask for and answer questions about proposal as they come up?

_____

_____

_____

_____

_____

_____

THE CLOSE PROCESS

The close process is not a knock-out punch, a manipulative technique, or a magical event. It is simply the culmination of doing a lot of work correctly that results in a new business relationship.

1. **What are buy-signals?** List examples of some you have observed. Next to those, list what you say or do when you hear a buy-signal?

_____

_____

_____

_____

_____

_____

_____

_____

_____

_____

_____

_____

_____

2. **When do you typically begin to close the sale?** Why is it advisable to ask for the business shortly after you have made the proposal and answered the prospect's questions?

_____

_____

_____

_____

_____

_____

3. **What are some non-manipulative ways to ask for the order?** If the buyers have signaled that they are interested in what you are offering, what you should say next?

_____

_____

_____

_____

_____

_____

4. **What can you do to close the sale if the prospects remain undecided?** What questions can you ask to improve your chancing of closing without begging or being excessively persistent?

_____

_____

_____

_____

_____

_____

5. **What is "selling the problem"and how can it help you close more sales?** What questions can you ask to cause prospects to state what might happen if they do not buy solve the agreed to problems? Have the prospect discuss in their own words what might happen if they don't make a decision, whether with you or someone else, soon.

_____

_____

_____

_____

_____

_____

_____

6. **If you find you cannot close the sale, make a list of the objections that you couldn't neutralize.**

_____

_____

_____

_____

_____

_____

_____

_____

_____

_____

_____

_____

_____

7. **Now prepare constructive statements to neutralize, if not eliminate, the objections that you have heard.** Practice your responses. Don't be surprised if new objections occur based on new economic or competitive reasons. Remember, it is not necessary to overcome every objection to close the sale.

_____

_____

_____

_____

_____

_____

_____

_____

_____

_____

_____

_____

_____

_____

8. **Of the eleven principles of selling (Chapter 10), which ones are most relevant to your situation.** If some are not applicable, why not?

_____

_____

_____

_____

_____

_____

_____

_____

_____

_____

_____

_____

_____

_____

_____

_____

_____

9. Once the prospect agrees to hire you, what are your next steps?
Experienced professionals are prepared to succeed; that is why they have contracts, letters of agreement, and other required documents ready for signature. What papers must you have ready to finalize your sale?

_____

_____

_____

_____

_____

_____

_____

_____

_____

_____

_____

_____

_____

Attract Sell Keep: The Workbook

ASK: A Roadmap to Attract, Sell, Keep

Section 3: Keep

Keeping customers can no longer be assumed. Today's service professionals must view each satisfied customer as a valued partner. Staying in contact and building long term relationships is a business skill well worth learning and practicing. It can lead to repeat business, referrals, financial security, and real friendships. Most importantly it is far easier to sell more services to satisfied customers than to develop new business. This growing list of loyal, satisfied customers is one of the assets potential business buyers will analyze to determine what they will pay for your business.

EXERCISES for Retaining the Customers You Want to Keep

1. **How do you currently keep track of your customers and prospects?**
    If you are not already using some form of customer relationship man-
    agement (CRM) software, start doing so. It is an essential marketing tool.

    _____

    _____

    _____

    _____

    _____

    _____

2. **What customer information do you normally collect?** Do you know:
    how the buyer discovered you; if you have thanked the referrer; if you
    have kept detail contact information, or what services you provided?
    Such information is pure gold and worth keeping.

    _____

    _____

    _____

    _____

    _____

    _____

3. Is the information you have about customers organized and easily accessible for marketing purposes? Is it protected and backed-up?

_____

_____

_____

_____

_____

_____

_____

4. How do you stay in contact and nurture your most profitable and loyal customers and referral sources each year?

_____

_____

_____

_____

_____

_____

5. **List the ways you can make sure your customers are satisfied with the services you provided.** Customer satisfaction is the cornerstone of customer loyalty.

_____

_____

_____

_____

_____

_____

6. **List the procedures, guarantees, or other remedial action you will take if a customer is dissatisfied.** It is essential that you have a policy in writing that your associates can refer to should such a situation arise.

_____

_____

_____

_____

_____

_____

7. **Describe ways you plan to maintain and increase customer loyalty each year.**

_____

_____

_____

_____

_____

_____

_____

8. **List strategies to prompt former customers to return after using your competitors.**

_____

_____

_____

_____

_____

_____

9. **How can you actively encourage satisfied customers, family members, and friends to refer prospects to you?** Referring business to them is a major one.

_____

_____

_____

_____

_____

_____

_____

_____

10. **Analyze current referral sources.** Are there any common characteristics that might permit you to concentrate your efforts on finding more of them?

_____

_____

_____

_____

_____

_____

11. **What would motivate someone to be an enthusiastic advocate of your services?**

_____

_____

_____

_____

_____

_____

12. **How can you help an enthusiastic referral source become more effective in screening out inappropriate prospects without offending them?**

_____

_____

_____

_____

_____

_____

_____

_____

13. **List at least ten people who are centers-of-influence in your community that might have opportunities to send business your way.** For example, if you are a psychologist interested in helping younger people shed their addictions, you might contact the principal of the local high school or college, members of your local police force, or bartenders.

\
\
\
\
\
\

14. **What can you do to generate referrals *for your natural allies*?** How can you become a respected source of information about qualified professionals in other fields?

\
\
\
\
\
\

15. **What can you say to the source of an undesirable referral without discouraging future business?**

_____

_____

_____

_____

_____

_____

16. **When someone asks you to refer a service provider, list the steps you take before making such a recommendation.** Why is this your ethical responsibility?

_____

_____

_____

_____

_____

_____

_____

17. Why is limiting your suggestions to one or two referrals enough?

_____

_____

_____

_____

_____

_____

18. Under what circumstances is it more advisable and ethical to make no recommendations or referrals?

_____

_____

_____

_____

_____

_____

_____

Attract Sell Keep: The Workbook

19. **How would you rate yourself in terms of managing your time effectively?** What actions might you take to keep yourself focused on attending to those tasks that only you can or want to perform? Do you know how to "unplug" to avoid the constant interruption of instant messaging, texts, emails, and phone calls?

_____

_____

_____

_____

_____

_____

20. **Analyze your financial circumstances to determine if you can hire one or more people to absorb some of the tasks you are now performing.** If so prepare a detailed job description and begin recruiting the right person(s) to fill the job.

_____

_____

_____

_____

_____

21. List the benefits and potential downside of hiring new associates.
Describe what tasks you would like to offload to free up your time for more productive and satisfying activities. What aspect of your current work do you want to retain?

22. **List ways you stay abreast of what is happening in your industry, both locally and elsewhere.** Are you a member of your industry's professional association? Do you attend at least one meeting per year?

Attract Sell Keep: The Workbook

ASK: A Roadmap to Attract, Sell, Keep

Section 4: Preparing Your Exit

The Best Time to Sell your business is when someone is very eager to buy it. When you are starting and growing your business, exiting it may be the furthest thing from your mind. But it is never too early to plan for what might be a bonanza.

EXERCISES for Making a Timely, Profitable Exit

1. **Periodically estimate the current value of your business and learn what you can do to maximize its sale.** Ask your lawyer, accountant, or other respected adviser for names of consultants who can advise you regarding the sale of your specific business.

_____

_____

_____

_____

_____

_____

_____

_____

_____

_____

_____

_____

2. **Make a list of the types and/or names of companies or individuals who might be good candidates for purchasing your business.** Meet and keep in touch with them. This may speed the process of selling your business when you are ready.

3. **What other exit alternatives are there beyond outright sale that you might consider?** Consider merger, incremental sale to associates, and Employee Stock Ownership Plan (ESOP), among others.

_____

_____

_____

_____

_____

_____

_____

_____

_____

_____

_____

_____

4. Describe a strategy to incrementally relinquish control and ownership of your company while insuring that your valued associates and customers can replace you without any detriment to the company's value.

_____

_____

_____

_____

_____

_____

_____

_____

_____

_____

_____

_____

_____

_____

In Conclusion

That is it. I hope these exercises were helpful in making you think more deeply about important matters pertaining to your career.

Feel free to send comments, questions, or suggestions of other exercises. My goal is to help ambitious, hard working professionals get the information they need to build a sustainable, growing, and enjoyable businesses.

Good luck,
Henry A. Feldman, Jr.
www.theaskbook.com

www.ingramcontent.com/pod-product-compliance
Lightning Source LLC
Chambersburg PA
CBHW071620170526
45166CB00003B/1134